THE STANDARD RESPONSE PROTOCOL

K12

Operational Guidance for Implementing The Standard Response Protocol In a K12 Environment

K12 SCHOOLS AND DISTRICTS

HOLD　　**SECURE**　　**LOCKDOWN**　　**EVACUATE**　　**SHELTER**

PEACE

It does not mean to be in a place where there is no noise, trouble, or hard work.

It means to be in the midst of those things and still be calm in your heart.

STANDARD RESPONSE PROTOCOL®
SRP 2023 K-12 CHANGE HISTORY VERSION 4.1

AUTHOR/CONTRIBUTOR	VERSION	REVISION DATE	REVISION COMMENTARY
John-Michael Keyes	1.0	2009-03-02	Original content
Russ Deffner John-Michael Keyes	2.0	2015-01-08	Version update. See: The Standard Response Protocol V2 An Overview of What's New in the SRP
Tom Kelley (TxSSC)	2.1	2017-12-02	Content, edits, formal inclusion of the Standard Response Protocol Extended "Hold in your classroom". Texas School Safety Center version
John-Michael Keyes	2.2	2018-05-22	Content, edits. Colorado School District Self Insurance Pool version.
John-Michael Keyes	3.0	2019-06-05	Incorporated "Hold in your classroom or area" into the Standard Response Protocol
John-Michael Keyes	4.0	2020-01-17	Replaced Lockout Action with Secure Action
Ellen Stoddard-Keyes	4.0	2020-06-23	Added new content and incorporated suggestions.
I Love U Guys Foundation	4.1	2022-6-15	Additional Guidance, Detail and Resources

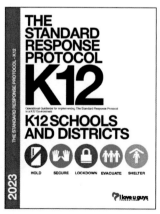

The Standard Response Protocol 2023 K12
Operational Guidance for Schools, Districts, Departments and Agencies

Version 4.1 ISBN-13: 978-1-951260-07-1

DEDICATION

On September 27th, 2006 a gunman entered Platte Canyon High School in Bailey, Colorado, held seven girls hostage and ultimately shot and killed Emily Keyes. During the time she was held hostage, Emily sent her parents text messages... "I love you guys" and "I love u guys. k?"

Emily's kindness, spirit, fierce joy, and the dignity and grace that followed this tragic event define the core of The "I Love U Guys" Foundation. This book is dedicated to Emily.

FORWARD

The original concept of this program came from recognizing that most school safety plans focused on response to individual incidents. Since there is no way to predict every single type of incident, that method leaves gaps in response. It is fairly common, after a tragedy, to hear someone say "I didn't think that would happen here," so the assumption is that there was no response plan for it.

Many safety plans The Foundation looked at contained similar actions being used for the various incidents, but they were called different things. The Standard Response Protocol was developed with input from many safety practitioners and is action-based, defining each physical response. When the actions are practiced and understood, they can be used almost universally for any incident. This is a life skill that stretches far beyond school.

This book contains guidance on using the actions, as well as discussions and other considerations when using The Standard Response Protocol.

ACKNOWLEDGMENTS

The Keyes family is primarily grateful to responders Deputy Chief A.J. DeAndrea and Deputy Mike Denuzzi for opening the door for discussion and communication in the aftermath of the tragedy, and to former investigative reporter Paula Woodward for making the introduction. (There's a story there...)

Thanks to Ted Zocco-Hochhalter for introducing us to emergency management for safer schools, and to Katherine Zocco-Hochhalter for bringing humanity to the conversation, and to both for sharing their knowledge and friendship.

STAFF

Need we say more? At the release of this version, The Foundation employs five people full time, all of whom bring unique skills, curiosity and intelligence to these materials, so it's all hands on deck.

Current Staff:

Allyson Jones, Communications Manager, Carly Posey, Mission Director, Dan Rector, Emergency Management Planner, Ellen Stoddard-Keyes, Operations Director, and John-Michael Keyes, Executive Director

BOARD OF DIRECTORS

Chris Zimmerman, Craig Straw, Dave Bauer, Frank DeAngelis, Heilit Biehl, James Englert, Louis S. Gonzalez, Martha Vargas, Murphy Robinson, and Pat Hamilton.

Whereas many nonprofits have a combative relationship with their Boards, we have always treasured ours for their dedication and wisdom.

AUTHORS AND CONTRIBUTORS

We are incredibly grateful to the people who have helped with the development of the programs. For contributions to content we are grateful to the following people:

Dr. David Benke (former teacher and former Board member) for Teacher Guidance;

Kevin Burd (Detective Lieutenant Ret., Priority of Life Training and Consulting) for content contribution and training expertise;

Russell Deffner (Advisor/Contractor/Volunteer) for Incident Command Guidance;

Tom Kelley (School Safety Training and Education Specialist, Texas School Safety Center) for content contributions;

Ian Lopez (Director of Safety & Security, Cherry Creek Schools) for content contribution;

John McDonald (Executive Director, Safety, Security and Emergency Planning, Jefferson County Public Schools) for ongoing discussion and input on what's really going on in the world;

Joleen Reefe (City and County of Broomfield Ret.) for the phrase, "Locks, Lights, Out of Sight";

Jaclyn Schildkraut (PhD, Associate Professor, Department of Criminal Justice, State University of New York at Oswego) for accuracy and research on drill and guidance;

Heidi Walts (Commander, Northglenn Police Department) for being the best sister and sister-in-law to John-Michael and Ellen, and also giving excellent guidance when they needed it the most.

ADJUNCT INSTRUCTORS

They conduct trainings around the country on a part time basis, bringing their expertise and knowledge to the table. And they bring back information about how we can improve the programs

Current Adjunct Instructors:

Stacy Avila (Arvada Police Dept. Ret.)

David Benke, retired teacher and former Board member

Kevin Burd (Detective Lieutenant Ret., Priority of Life Training and Consulting)

Pat Hamilton (Chief Operating Officer, Adams 12 Five Star Schools)

Chris Zimmerman (Principal, Cimarron Middle School, Douglas County)

CONTACT INFORMATION

The "I Love U Guys" Foundation can be reached online at https://iloveuguys.org.

Email: srp@iloveuguys.org

The "I Love U Guys" Foundation
PO Box 919, Conifer, CO 80433
303.426.3100

"Tactics are intel driven."

What we plan is based on what we know.

"But the environment dictates tactics."

But what we do, is based on where we are.

– Deputy Chief A.J. DeAndrea
– Civilian Translation: John-Michael Keyes

TABLE OF CONTENTS

MISSION

The "I Love U Guys" Foundation was created to restore and protect the joy of youth through educational programs and positive actions in collaboration with families, schools, communities, organizations and government entities.

THE "I LOVE U GUYS" FOUNDATION

On September 27th, 2006 a gunman entered Platte Canyon High School in Bailey, Colorado, held seven girls hostage and ultimately shot and killed Emily Keyes. During the time she was held hostage, Emily sent her parents text messages... "I love you guys" and "I love u guys. k?"

Emily's kindness, spirit, fierce joy, and the dignity and grace that followed this tragic event define the core of The "I Love U Guys" Foundation.

COMMITMENT

There are several things we are committed to. The most important thing we can do is offer our material at no cost to schools, districts, departments, agencies and organizations. The reason we are able to continue to provide this service is due, in part, to the generosity of our donors and Mission Partners (see Partner with Love on the website). The "I Love U Guys" Foundation works very hard to keep our costs down as well as any costs associated with our printed materials. Donor and Mission Partner support allows us to stretch those dollars and services even more. Your gift, no matter the size, helps us achieve our mission. Your help makes a difference to the students, teachers, first responders, and the communities in which we live and work.

WARNINGS AND DISCLAIMER

Every effort has been made to make this book as complete and accurate as possible, but no warranty or fitness is implied. The information provided is on an "as is" basis. Please visit our website (https://iloveuguys.org) for the detailed information.

There are some links to resources in this book. In most PDFs they will be clickable, but The Foundation cannot guarantee that the actual source is still available at that site.

COPYRIGHTS AND TRADEMARKS

In order to protect the integrity and consistency of The Standard Response Protocol, The "I Love U Guys" Foundation exercises all protection under copyright and trademark. Use of this material is governed by the Terms of Use (details in the MOU and NOI documents) or a Commercial Licensing Agreement.

COMMERCIAL LICENSING

Incorporating the SRP into a commercial product, like software or publication, requires a commercial license. Please contact The "I Love U Guys" Foundation for more information and costs.

ABOUT SRP 2023

Since 2015, The Foundation offered optional classroom training that included "Hold in your classroom." In 2017, The Foundation developed materials for The Standard Response Protocol Extended (SRP-X) that included the Hold action.

With SRP 2021, the Hold action was incorporated into the Standard Response Protocol and the Lockout action was changed to Secure.

For SRP 2023, there is expanded guidance, the introduction of the "SRP Lockdown Drill," and new communications guidance.

Although the SRP 2021 version is still valid, The "I Love U Guys" Foundation recommends updating to the newer version as soon as feasible.

As you begin to implement and drill the protocol, keep in mind that environments are different. What that means is that we provide you with some tactics. Things we know. But your school, your agencies, and your environment, will ultimately dictate what you do.

THE "I LOVE U GUYS" FOUNDATION MOU

Some schools, districts, departments and agencies may desire a formalized Memorandum of Understanding (MOU) with The "I Love U Guys" Foundation. For a current version of the MOU, please visit iloveuguys.org.

The purpose of an MOU is to define responsibilities of each party and provide scope, and clarity of expectations. It affirms agreement of stated protocol by schools, districts, departments and agencies. It also confirms the online availability of the Foundation's materials.

An additional benefit for the Foundation is in seeking funding. Some private grantors view the MOU as a demonstration of program effectiveness.

This can be emailed to srp@iloveuguys.org

NOTICE OF INTENT

Another option is to formally notify the Foundation with a Notice of Intent (NOI). This is a notice that you are reviewing the materials but have not adopted them yet. This is also available on the website.

At a minimum, schools, districts, departments and agencies that will ultimately incorporate the SRP into their safety plans and practices should email srp@iloveuguys.org and let us know.

FAIR USE POLICY

PRIVACY POLICY

TERMS OF USE

Schools, districts, departments, agencies and organizations may use these materials, at no cost, under the following conditions:

1. Materials are not re-sold
2. Core actions and directives are not modified
    2.1. **Hold** - "In Your Room or Area."
    2.2. **Secure** - "Get Inside, Lock Outside Doors"
    2.3. **Lockdown** - "Locks, Lights, Out of Sight"
    2.4. **Evacuate** - A Location may be specified
    2.5. **Shelter** - State the Hazard and the Safety Strategy
3. The Notification of Intent (NOI) is used when the materials are being evaluated. A sample NOI can be downloaded from the website, and is provided to The "I Love U Guys" Foundation through one of the following:
    3.1. Complete the NOI and email it to srp@iloveuguys.org
    3.2. Send an email to srp@iloveuguys.org
4. The Memorandum of Understating (MOU) is used when it has been determined that the materials will be used. A sample MOU can be downloaded from iloveuguys.org, and is provided to The "I Love U Guys" Foundation by emailing it to srp@iloveuguys.org
5. The following modifications to the materials are allowable:
    5.1. Localization of Evacuation events
    5.2. Localization of Shelter events
    5.3. Addition of organization logo

ONE DEMAND

The protocol also carries an obligation. Kids and teens are smart. An implicit part of the SRP is that authorities and school personnel tell students what's going on.

Certainly, temper it at the elementary school level, but middle schoolers and older need accurate information for the greatest survivability, and to minimize panic and assist recovery.

Note: Student training includes preparation for some alternative methods during a tactical response but reinforces deference to local law enforcement.

REQUEST FOR COMMENT

The Standard Response Protocol is a synthesis of common practices in use at a number of districts, departments and agencies. The evolution of SRP has included review, comment and suggestion from a number of practitioners. With each version, the SRP is subjected to tactical scrutiny by law enforcement agencies, and operational review and adoption by schools. Suggestions for modification can be made via email at srp_rfc@iloveuguys.org. Please include contact information, district, department or agency, including daytime phone.

STANDARD RESPONSE PROTOCOL®

INTRODUCTION

This document outlines The Standard Response Protocol (SRP) and offers guidance on incorporating this protocol into a school safety plan for critical incident response within individual schools in a school district.

The intent of this document is to provide basic guidance with respect to local conditions and authorities. The only mandate presented is that districts, agencies and departments retain the "Terms of Art, which are actions," and "Directives" defined by this protocol.

The SRP is not a replacement for any school safety plan or program. It is simply a classroom response enhancement for critical incidents, designed to provide consistent, clear, shared language and actions among all students, staff and first responders.

As a standard, SRP is being adopted by emergency managers, law enforcement, school and district administrators and emergency medical services across the country. Hundreds of agencies have evaluated it and recommended the SRP to thousands of schools across the US and Canada.

New materials and updates can be found online at
https://iloveuguys.org/The-Standard-Response-Protocol.html#Intro

A CRITICAL LOOK

Be prepared to look at existing plans with a critical eye, as often they can be described as a "Directive" of a certain "Term of Art." For example, conducting a fire drill is practicing a specific type of evacuation and the actions performed are similar in all evacuation scenarios. It makes sense to teach and train broader evacuation techniques while testing or practicing a more specific directive, like evacuating to the parking lot due to a fire.

TIME BARRIERS

Time barriers or measures taken beforehand to 'harden the structure' can be an invaluable asset to safety; not only for staff and students, but also visitors to a campus who expect a friendly and secure environment.

Time barriers are best described as a physical barrier that slows down the entry into, or movement through, a facility. Any additional delay allows trained persons to take further protective action and gives first responders more time to arrive.

An example of a time barrier is making the exterior doors of a building automatically lock, and could include installing a film on glass door panels to prevent them from shattering, thereby delaying an intruder's attempt to break into the premises.

THE POWER OF A LOCKED DOOR

Finally, the most powerful time barrier in an active assailant event is a locked classroom door. The Sandy Hook Advisory Commission Report* says this:

"The testimony and other evidence presented to the Commission reveals that there has never been an event in which an active shooter breached a locked classroom door."

In Foundation investigations of past school shootings where life was lost behind a locked classroom door, some edge cases were revealed. The perpetrator in the Red Lake, MN incident gained entry into the classroom by breaking through the side panel window next to the classroom door. In the Platte Canyon hostage incident, the perpetrator was already in the room when Jeffco Regional SWAT explosively breached the classroom door. At Marjory Stoneman Douglas High School, shots were fired through glass panels in doors, but the perpetrator never entered any locked classrooms.

> "SRP is not a replacement... it's an enhancement to your existing safety plans."

BEFORE YOU BEGIN

Districts and schools typically have a comprehensive safety program established and executed by a dedicated team of safety or security personnel. That same Safety Team should be responsible for incorporating the SRP into the safety plan. Including staff, students and a counselor or nurse on the Safety Team can greatly increase the buy-in and participation from all campus safety stakeholders.

If it was not done during the development of the existing safety plan it is highly encouraged that, while incorporating the SRP, the safety team establish contact with local emergency services and law enforcement officials as they can help ensure safety plans will not conflict with existing local emergency services protocols.

*FINAL REPORT OF THE SANDY HOOK ADVISORY COMMISSION
Presented to Governor Dannel P. Malloy State of Connecticut
March 6, 2015 - Document page 238 - Appendix A-I.1

HOLD   **SECURE**   **LOCKDOWN**   **EVACUATE**   **SHELTER**

THE STANDARD RESPONSE PROTOCOL

A critical ingredient in the safe school recipe is the uniform classroom response to an incident at school. Weather events, fires, accidents, intruders and other threats to student safety are scenarios that are planned and trained for by school and district administration and staff.

Historically, schools have taken a scenario-based approach to respond to hazards and threats. It's not uncommon to find a stapled sheaf of papers or tabbed binder in a teacher's desk that describes a variety of things that might happen, and the specific response to each event.

SRP IS ACTION BASED

The Standard Response Protocol is based not on individual scenarios but on the response to any given scenario. Like the Incident Command System (ICS), SRP demands a specific vocabulary but also allows for great flexibility. The premise is simple: there are five specific actions that can be performed during an incident. When communicating these actions, each is followed by a "Directive." Execution of the action is performed by active participants, including students, staff, teachers and first responders.

- **Hold** is followed by "In your Room or Area. Clear the Halls" and is the protocol used when the hallways need to be kept clear of people.

- **Secure** is followed by "Get Inside, Lock Outside Doors" and is the protocol used to safeguard students and staff within the building.

- **Lockdown** is followed by "Locks, Lights, Out of Sight" and is the protocol used to secure individual rooms and keep students quiet and in place.

- **Evacuate** may be followed by a location, and is the protocol used to move students and staff from one location to a different location in or out of the building.

- **Shelter** is always followed by the hazard and a safety strategy and is the protocol for group and self-protection.

These specific actions can act as both a verb and a noun. If the action is Lockdown, it would be announced on public address as "Lockdown! Locks, Lights, Out of Sight." Communication to local responders would then be "We are in Lockdown."

ACTIONS

Each response has specific student and staff actions. The Evacuate action might be followed by a location: "Evacuate to the Bus Zone." Actions can be chained. For instance, "Evacuate to Hallway. Shelter for Earthquake. Drop, Cover and Hold."

BENEFITS

The benefits of SRP become quickly apparent. By standardizing the vocabulary, all stakeholders can understand the response and status of the event. For students, this provides continuity of expectations and actions throughout their educational career. For teachers, this becomes a simpler process to train and drill. For first responders, the common vocabulary and protocols establish a greater predictability that persists through the duration of an incident. Parents can easily understand the practices and can reinforce the protocol. Additionally, this protocol enables rapid response determination when an unforeseen event occurs.

The protocol also allows for a more predictable series of actions as an event unfolds. An intruder event may start as a Lockdown, but as the intruder is isolated, first responders may assist as parts of the school "Evacuate to a different building," and later "Evacuate to the bus zone."

TACTICAL RESPONSES

SRP also acknowledges that some school incidents involve a tactical response from law enforcement, and suggests consultation with local law enforcement regarding expectations and actions.

SEQUENCING THE ACTIONS

As you read through the Action Sections, you'll see that the actions can be sequenced as situations change and information is gathered. See page 29 for examples of how this can, and has, been done.

STANDARD RESPONSE PROTOCOL®

CONSIDERATIONS, AND HOW TO BEGIN

This section of the guidance gives references for building and progressing your Emergency Operations Plan. It defines conditions, actions, responsibilities and other aspects of preparing and incorporating The Standard Response Protocol within a school or district safety plan.

EMERGENCY OPERATIONS PLAN

To create or review your EOP, a good resource is the Readiness and Emergency Management for Schools Technical Assistance Center.

Go to rems.ed.gov. Click the Tools button, and in the dropdown menu, choose K12 Emergency Management Virtual Toolkit.

PREREQUISITES:
NIMS AND ICS

In order to coordinate the use of the SRP in district plans, it is highly recommended that key individuals within the district and those with a role in district/campus emergency operations, complete the following courses through FEMA.

1. IS 100.C: Introduction to the Incident Command System
2. IS-700.B: An Introduction to the National Incident Management System
3. IS 362.A: Multihazard Emergency Planning for Schools

These courses are available online at no cost on the internet at http://training.fema.gov. Anticipate one to three hours per course to successfully achieve certification. The courses are offered at no charge. Please note: The "I Love U Guys" Foundation is not affiliated with FEMA.

RESOURCES AND CREATING RELATIONSHIPS

Throughout this book, you'll see suggestions to contact local or regional responders. Whether it's law enforcement, emergency services, the fire department, or your county emergency manager, communication with these local resources is essential.

In most areas, schools are the largest population centers during a school day, so it makes sense to utilize the advice and services those agencies provide. Additionally, some county emergency managers are equipped to assist with your safety planning. Some school districts are able to engage with their regional Department of Homeland Security for training resources.

Take a look around your county and state and see what's available.

If you would like to speak with other schools or districts prior to utilizing the Standard Response Protocol, contact The " I Love U Guys" Foundation at info@iloveuguys.org and we may be able to connect you with a school or district near you that has a similar profile and/or similar challenges.

TALK TO THE FIRE MARSHAL

It's important to discuss classroom security options and modifications with local fire authorities. Some will allow a locked classroom door to be propped open during the school day, while some will not. Variances in local Fire Codes and applications will help determine the options for your schools.

DOORS, LOCKS AND STRESS

A consistent observation by first responders is that human beings have difficulty completing even routine tasks when they are under stress. The otherwise simple task of locking the classroom door may become extremely difficult for a teacher who has just heard a Lockdown order. Elevated adrenaline levels may result in the loss of fine motor skills, which can impede an act as normal as inserting a key to lock a door.

If your classroom doors cannot be locked using gross motor skills from the inside of the classroom, keeping the classroom doors locked during instruction has proven to be a time barrier. While this may create an inconvenience if students are late or need to re-enter the classroom for other reasons, it provides an essential layer of protection against intruders.

STANDARD RESPONSE PROTOCOL®

WHO STARTS?

For obvious reasons, a person in authority at the school or district level would have to approve the use of the SRP. While they may be the authority, however, it's usually a security person or someone from the safety team (Liaison) who actually initiates the process.

If the organization has an MOU with The "I Love U Guys" Foundation that person is the Authorized Liaison, meaning that we communicate directly with them about updates and new materials.

Either way, the Liaison is the person who organizes and schedules internal training, puts up posters, and plans for outward communication. They may engage the district communication person to plan messages to educate parents and the community on the SRP.

MEMORANDA OF UNDERSTANDING

Establishing a Memorandum of Understanding (MOU) and/or Mutual Aid Agreement (MAA) between responding agencies and local resources is critical. It is insufficient to rely on a conversation or handshake between entities who would respond to an incident or provide resources during an emergency.

Written agreements such as MOUs and MAAs are important to emergency operation plans and should be reviewed and updated regularly.

An SRP-focused Sample MOU between a School District and Law Enforcement/Fire/EMS was created in order to guide schools in creating effective MOUs with local first responders. Download it from the SRP section at https://iloveuguys.org

TRAINING RESOURCES
SRP Training

While the SRP materials may be downloaded and implemented at no cost, The Foundation can provide onsite or online training for a cost, and has worked with a number of organizations in providing training workshops.

Send training inquiries to training@iloveuguys.org.

Do-It-Yourself Training

The "I Love U Guys" Foundation also provides a number of print, video, and presentation materials which can be downloaded.

It is recommended that a refresher training be conducted for students and staff in schools at least once during the school year using the materials. This can be as easy as showing a 7-minute video. Check https://iloveuguys.org frequently for new and updated materials.

WHAT ABOUT PARENTS AND GUARDIANS?

The Foundation provides informational SRP handouts for schools to send home or email to parents. These describe the SRP actions and directives, and also let parents know what they should expect to see and do during and after an incident.

While it's important to make sure parents understand this outward-facing part of your safety plan, finding the best method to deliver the information can be challenging. Here are some ways schools communicate the SRP to parents:

* Back to school events

* Email a link to the parent handout from the school website twice a year. That can be accompanied by student lessons on SRP.

* Flyers at parent teacher conferences

* A short training on Back to School night

* School Accountability Committee safety procedure review

* One district we're aware of publishes a short magazine periodically to send to the parents with school information. They put in a 2-page spread on the SRP, along with articles about what's going on at the school.

MESSAGING
Email, Text, and Auto Dialer

COMMUNICATION

Every school's Emergency Operations Plan (EOP) should contain a section for communicating both internally and externally during a crisis situation.

In any type of incident, clear and well-planned communication is essential. Depending on the type of incident, you might have only minutes to prepare a statement and communicate it to the appropriate people.

Primarily, give the students and staff as much information as possible so they can make informed decisions about their actions. If little is known about the situation, tell them that.

Communication to parents and guardians is critical as well. It's likely that a number of them will show up at the school no matter what's going on, so letting them know what's happening and what to do is a must.

INCIDENT COMMAND

When your Safety Team is creating an EOP, they'll include some level of the Incident Command System (ICS), which is the hierarchy of authority and responsibilities. One role in ICS is the Public Information Officer (PIO) and this role can be used on a daily basis.

Having a Communication Team in your school and/or district is good practice in order to keep lines of communication ongoing for everyday events and activities.

Many school districts have a full-time Communication/PIO supervisor. Within a school, there is usually at least one person who manages the low-level event and activity communication along with their primary job.

High-level event information should be as clear, concise, and complete as possible. Create a policy for protocol and content for each communication channel to maintain consistency.

DIRECT COMMUNICATION

It is safe to assume that most schools/districts communicate regularly with the student families through email.

In an emergency, add alternate methods for communication such as text and phone, which aren't used as frequently. Doing so will alert the recipients that this is more important than daily communication.

Decide which methods of direct communication are the best fit for your community. This is reliant on your community's internet bandwidth, cell phone service and other preferences. Whatever you choose needs to be reliable, fast, and reach a high percentage of the community members.

SOCIAL MEDIA CHANNELS

Most school day disruptions don't require any social media engagement, but if it is beneficial to alert the community of an incident, decide which channels are the best fit for your community. This is reliant on internet bandwidth, cell phone service and other preferences. Whatever you choose needs to be reliable, fast, and reach a high percentage of the community members. Document who on the Communication Team has access to update each channel.

The team should pre-script some basic messages that may be sent out, with blank spaces for details like time and date. Having these pre-approved and available will aid the team later if they're under stress or time constraints.

CONTACTS

After determining the best methods to use, decide who you will need to communicate with in each situation. Certainly staff and parents, but also students depending on the age group. Asking parents to keep their contact information updated is critical. Add responders, dispatchers and media contacts as needed.

TIME

For certain incidents, there are only a few minutes to prepare. If Law Enforcement or Fire is involved, people will hear about an incident quickly. Reaching your stakeholders immediately with any type of message acknowledging the incident is essential. Have some basic message formats pre-approved and ready to use.

CONTENT

Not every situation needs immediate text messages and emails, so it's important to determine what is warranted and when. Less urgent situations—a school cancellation with ample notice, for example—might warrant an email, mass phone message and website update, whereas an unexpected early dismissal requires mass phone calls and text messages to ensure that information is received quickly.

An initial message can be as simple as stating that something has happened, and telling stakeholders where to find updates.

Include only the factual information you have; do not speculate. The recipients of your outgoing messages must be able to trust in the validity of the content.

Any situation that requires emergency communication for an incident will also require a follow-up.

If the school or district has a web page with information about what each SRP Action means and what the directives are, include a link to that page.

Plan on how you will be providing updates if those are needed, and include a link or reference to that site so recipients know where to look.

 ## SAMPLE MESSAGING FOR EACH SRP ACTION

The following sections contain detailed instructions and considerations for each of the Standard Response Protocol Actions. Each section has sample messaging for that specific Action, and when and how it can be used.

FREQUENCY

Not all Actions will require an immediate communication response. For instance, if you anticipate a Hold or Secure taking no longer than 20 minutes, there's probably no need to alert anyone. If it looks like it will take longer, consider sending something out, since the situation has now become a bigger disruption to the day.

PREPARATION

A tabletop exercise is a start; basically, it's a brainstorming session. Your Communication Team can talk through possible scenarios and formulate messaging accordingly. Think about what immediate information is necessary, how to follow up, and who they will need to speak with/follow to receive trusted updates.

The team should pre-script some basic messages that may be sent out, with blank spaces for details like time and date. Having these pre-approved and available will aid the team later if they're under stress or time constraints.

TWO MINDS

There are different messaging philosophies regarding how much information is too much information. In some events, a detailed description of the SRP Action and the steps taken by the school in response to the event are warranted. Guidance for this type of communication can be found under "Messaging to Parents" in the Hold, Secure, Lockdown, Evacuate, and Shelter sections.

For other events, a more generic message may provide enough information. The goal of the generic message is to inform the broader community that one of the SRP Actions was implemented but that no further action is required on their part. Think of it as a way to put parents, guardians, and others at ease.

Alternatively, the generic message can be used immediately following the protocol activation if details are unknown. In that case, a statement that "more information will be sent out via *(insert a link to them to click on)*."

GENERIC STANDARD RESPONSE PROTOCOL MESSAGE TO PARENTS

Subject: Safety Notification - [School Name] Activated a Standard Response Protocol

Dear Parent or Guardian,

Today the Standard Response Protocol was activated at *[School Name]* due to *[state the reason(s) that you used the action(s) of the Standard Response Protocol]*.

The safety and security of your child are our top priority. Learn more about the Standard Response Protocol at iloveuguys.org/The-Standard-Response-Protocol.html

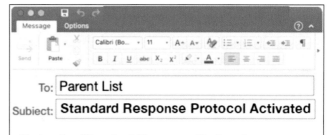

To: Parent List

Subject: **Standard Response Protocol Activated**

Today the Standard Response Protocol was activated at your students school due to criminal activity in the area. Students were not impacted and classes continued as usual.

The safety and security of your child are our top priority. Learn more about the Standard Response Protocol at iloveuguys.org

HOLD
In Your Room or Area

HOLD
IN YOUR ROOM OR AREA.

There are situations that require students and staff to remain in their classrooms or stay out of access areas. For example, an altercation in the hallway may require keeping students out of the halls until it is resolved. A medical issue may require only one area to be cleared, with halls still open in case outside medical assistance is required.

There may be a need for students who are not in a classroom to proceed to an area where they can be supervised and remain safe.

PUBLIC ADDRESS

The public address for Hold is: "Hold in your room or area. Clear the Halls." and is repeated twice each time the public address is performed. There may be a need to add directives for students that are not in a classroom, at lunch, or some other location where they should remain until the Hold is lifted.

"Hold in your room or area. Clear the Halls.
Hold in your room or area. Clear the Halls."

An example of a medical emergency would be:

"Students and staff, please Hold in the cafeteria or your room. We're attending to a medical situation near the office."

When it's been resolved:

"Students and staff, the Hold is released. All clear.

Thank you for your assistance in making this Hold work smoothly."

PUBLIC ADDRESS - RELEASE

A Hold Action can be released by Public Address.

"The Hold is released. All Clear.
The Hold is released. All Clear."

INCIDENT COMMAND SYSTEM

The School Incident Command System should be initiated.

ACTIONS

Students and teachers are to remain in their classroom or area, even if there is a scheduled class change until the all-clear is announced.

Students and staff in common areas, like a cafeteria or a gym, may be asked to remain in those areas or move to adjoining areas like a locker room.

Students and staff outside of the building should remain outside unless the administration directs otherwise.

It is suggested that prior to closing the classroom door, teachers should sweep the hallway for nearby students. Additionally, teachers should take attendance, note the time, and conduct classroom activities as usual.

In a high school with an open campus policy, communicate as much detail as possible to students who are temporarily off-campus.

RESPONSIBILITY

Typically an administrator is responsible for initiating a Hold. However, anyone should be able to call for a Hold if they observe something happening that would require this action.

PREPARATION

Student, teacher, and administrator training.

DRILLS

Hold should be drilled at least once a year, or as mandated by state requirements.

CONTINGENCIES

Students are trained that if they are not in a classroom they may be asked to identify the nearest classroom and join that class for the duration of the Hold.

EXAMPLES OF HOLD CONDITIONS

The following are some examples of when a school might initiate a Hold:

- An altercation in a hallway;
- A medical issue that needs attention;
- Unfinished maintenance operation in a common area during class changes.

SAMPLE OUTWARD MESSAGING TO PARENTS

This is a guide for outward messaging after a Hold action was used in the school. Usually, it is sent after a Hold is cleared. However if the Hold goes on for an extended period of time or it is happening close to release time, make sure to let the families know. Have a central digital platform that your public information team can easily update, and people can go to for information.

Variables in the message are in italic type.

Current Hold during the school day

Email

Subject Line: Safety Notification - Hold Currently Activated at *[School Name]*

Dear Parent or Guardian,

[School Name] has been placed in Hold due to *[state the reason for the Hold]*.

As a precaution, students and staff are asked to remain in their classrooms in order to keep the hallways empty. Classroom learning will continue throughout the Hold, but students will not be able to change classes.

The safety and security of your child is our top priority. We will continue to monitor the situation and update you further as soon as we have more information.

Watch for updates here *[link to the platform you'll be updating]*

What is a Hold Action? *

Current Hold at the end of the day

Email

Subject Line: Safety Notification - Hold Currently Activated at *[School Name]*

Dear Parent or Guardian,

[School Name] has been placed in Hold due to *[state the reason for the Hold]*.

As a precaution, students and staff are asked to remain in their classrooms in order to keep the hallways empty. Classroom learning will continue throughout the Hold, but students will not be able to leave until the situation is resolved.

Student dismissal may be delayed for a short time.
Please be patient.

The safety and security of your child is our top priority. We will continue to monitor the situation and update you further as soon as we have more information.

Watch for updates here *[link to the platform you'll be updating]*

What is a Hold Action? *

Text Message

[School Name] has been placed in Hold as a precaution. This situation may impact student dismissal. Please check your email for more information.

Phone Call

Parents, *[School Name]* has been placed in Hold due to *[state the reason for the Hold]*. As a precaution, we have placed the school in Hold to keep the halls empty. Student dismissal may be delayed for a short time. Please be patient. We will continue to monitor the situation and update you further as soon as we have more information.

Notification that a Hold occurred during the day

Email

Subject Line: Safety Notification - Hold Ended at *[School Name]*

Dear Parent or Guardian,

[School Name] was placed in Hold from *[start time]* to *[end time]* due to *[state the reason for the Hold]*.

As a precaution, students and staff were asked to remain in their classrooms in order to keep the hallways empty. Classroom learning continued throughout the Hold, and all school operations have returned to normal.

The safety and security of your child is our top priority. We will continue to keep you informed about important concerns at our school.

What is a Hold Action? *

* The Hold Action is used when the hallways in the school need to remain clear. Classroom learning will still take place as normal during a Hold, but students may not be able to change classes until after the Hold has been lifted.

Link to either your website or iloveuguys.org/The-Standard-Response-Protocol.html for them to learn more.

SECURE
Get inside Lock Outside Doors

SECURE
GET INSIDE, LOCK OUTSIDE DOORS.

The Secure Action is called when there is a threat or hazard outside of the school building. Whether it's due to violence or criminal activity in the immediate neighborhood, or a dangerous animal in the playground, Secure uses the security of the physical facility to act as protection.

PUBLIC ADDRESS

The public address for Secure is: "Secure! Get Inside. Lock outside doors" and is repeated twice each time the public address is performed.

"Secure! Get Inside, Lock outside doors.
Secure! Get Inside, Lock outside doors."

"Students and staff, the school is currently in the Secure Action due to *[cause]* in the neighborhood. No one is allowed in or out of the building at this time. Stay inside and continue with your day."

PUBLIC ADDRESS - RELEASE

A Secure Action can be released by Public Address.

"The Secure is released. All Clear.
The Secure is released. All Clear."

"Students and staff, the Secure is released. All clear. Thank you for your assistance with making this Secure work smoothly."

ACTIONS

The Secure Action demands bringing people into a secure building and locking all outside access points.

Where possible, classroom activities would continue uninterrupted. Classes being held outside would return to the building and, if possible, continue inside the building.

There may be occasions when students expect to be able to leave the building - end of classes, job commitment, etc. Depending on the condition, this may have to be delayed until the area is safe.

During the training period, it should be emphasized to students as well as their parents that they may be inconvenienced by these directives, but their cooperation is important to ensure their safety.

ADDING A LIFECYCLE TO THE SECURE PROTOCOL

As a situation evolves there may be more information available to guide decision making. With the Secure Protocol, there is the option to transition from the initial response of "No one in or out" to some access control.

NO ONE IN OR OUT

The initial directive and practice during the Secure Action is to retain students and staff within the building and prevent entry into the building.

CONTROLLED RELEASE

An unresolved, but not directly evident, situation at the end of the school day may warrant a Controlled Release. During a Controlled Release, parents or guardians may be asked to pick up students rather than have them walk home. Buses may run as normal, but increased monitoring of the bus area should occur. There may be additional law enforcement presence.

MONITORED ENTRY

When there is a perceived threat but it's not immediate, entrances may be attended by security or law enforcement and anyone entering the building is more closely monitored. Students and staff walking between buildings or going to the parking lot might be escorted with heightened awareness.

SCHOOL IS SECURED
MONITORED ENTRY AND CONTROLLED RELEASE

ESCUELA BAJO PROTECCIÓN
ENTRADA VIGILADA Y SALIDA CONTROLADA

INCIDENT COMMAND SYSTEM

The School Incident Command System should be initiated.

RESPONSIBILITY

During a Secure Action, administration or staff may be required to lock exterior access points. Staff members assigned "Primary Responsibility" for a "Secure Zone" would follow the designated protocol during a drill as well. These areas may include doorways, windows, loading docks, and fire escape ladder access points. The assigned staff is designated as having "Secure Duty."

A person should also be assigned "Secondary Responsibility" for Secure Duty in the event the person with Primary Responsibility is absent or unable to perform the protocol.

Assign someone to attach the Secure posters outfacing to building entry doors, alerting potential visitors of the Secure condition.

REPORTED BY

Secure is typically reported by local emergency dispatch to the school office. The office staff then invokes the public address and informs the administration.

It may also be reported by students, staff or teachers if a threat is directly observed outside of the building.

PREPARATION

Identification of perimeter access points that must be locked in a Secure Action defines the Perimeter. In the event a perimeter cannot be secured, identify areas within each building that can be secured.

Secure Zones - areas of a school or campus with exterior access points - should be established and protocols developed to ensure that those on "Secure Duty" attend to all areas in their zone.

Preparation includes identification of staff with Primary and Secondary responsibility and assignment of these duties.

DRILLS

Secure drills should be performed at least twice a year, or as mandated by state requirements. At least one should be performed while outdoor activities are in progress.

CONTINGENCIES

There may be physical attributes to the campus that mandate special handling of a Secure Action. An example would be a campus where modular buildings are present. If the modular building cannot be secured, it may be best for students to Evacuate to the main building rather than going to Secure in the modular building. Listen for specific additional directives.

If the school is a distributed campus (multiple permanent buildings), they will have to consider what their perimeter is. In a perceived and indirect threat, they may decide that extra supervision for class changes between buildings is sufficient and appropriate.

If during a Secure Action, an additional hazard manifests (i.e.: fire, flood, hazmat), then additional directives will be given for the appropriate response.

EXAMPLES OF SECURE CONDITIONS

The following are some examples of when a school or emergency dispatch might call for a Secure Action.

- An unknown or unauthorized person on the grounds
- Dangerous animal on or near the grounds
- Criminal activity in the area
- Planned police activity in the neighborhood

SECURE AND HOLD

Sometimes people become confused about the difference between "Secure" and "Hold." During a Hold, the halls are cleared, students remain in their classrooms with their teachers and business continues as usual. If people are outside, they remain outside. During a Secure, people are brought inside, and all activities inside the school continue as usual but no one will move in or out of the building. The main difference is that during a Secure the halls are open and may be utilized by students and staff as needed. People inside the school may not notice any difference in their daily routines during a Secure.

Remember, the main difference between the two is that a Secure is enacted when a threat or hazard is outside of the school. A Hold is used when there is a need for the halls to remain empty, meaning the issue is inside the building. During both instances, classroom instruction should continue as normal.

SECURE
Get inside Lock Outside Doors

SAMPLE OUTWARD MESSAGING TO PARENTS

This is a guide for outward messaging when a Secure Action is used in the school. Have a central digital platform that your public information team can easily update, and people can go to for information.

State in the message if the situation allows for Monitored Entry and Controlled Release. Variables are in italic type.

Current Secure Action during the school day

Email

Subject Line: Safety Notification - Secure Currently Activated at *[School Name]*

Dear Parent or Guardian,

[School Name] has been notified of *[state the activity occurring outside of the building]*. As a precaution, we have placed the school in Secure. During the Secure Action, all doors are locked and no one can leave or enter the building. *[Modify for monitored entry and controlled release]*

Watch for updates here *[link to the platform you'll be updating]*

What is the Secure Action? *

Current Secure Action at the end of the day

Email

Subject Line: Safety Notification - Secure Currently Activated at *[School Name]*

Dear Parent or Guardian,

[School Name] has been notified of *[state the activity occurring outside of the building]*. As a precaution, we have placed the school in Secure. During Secure, all doors are locked and no one can leave or enter the building. *[Modify for monitored entry and controlled release]*

Students may not be able to leave until the situation is resolved, and dismissal may be delayed for a short time. Please be patient.

Watch for updates here *[link to the platform you'll be updating]*

What is the Secure Action? *

Text Message

[School Name] is currently in Secure as a precaution. This situation has the potential to affect student dismissal. Please check your email for more information.

Phone Call

Parents, *[School Name]* has been notified of *[state the activity occurring outside of the building]*. As a precaution, we have placed the school in Secure.

Students may not be able to leave until the situation is resolved, and dismissal may be delayed for a short time. Please be patient.

Please check your email for more information.

Notification that school was in Secure Action

Email

Subject Line: Safety Notification - Secure Ended at [School Name]

Dear Parent or Guardian,

Today *[School Name]* was notified of *[state the activity occurring outside of the building]*. As a precaution, we placed the school in Secure. The Secure status lasted *[state the length of time in Secure]*. All school operations have now returned to normal.

What is the Secure Action? *

* The Secure Action is called when there is a threat or hazard outside of the school building. Secure uses the security of the physical facility to act as protection. During Secure, all students and staff are brought into the secure building and all exterior doors are locked. Classes are able to continue uninterrupted inside the building.

Link to either your website or iloveuguys.org/The-Standard-Response-Protocol.html for them to learn more.

LOCKDOWN
Locks, Lights, Out of Sight

LOCKDOWN
LOCKS, LIGHTS, OUT OF SIGHT

Lockdown is called when there is a threat or hazard inside the school building. From parental custody disputes to intruders to an active assailant, Lockdown uses classroom and school security actions to protect students and staff from the threat.

PUBLIC ADDRESS

The public address for Lockdown is: "Lockdown! Locks, Lights, Out of Sight!" and is repeated twice each time the public address is performed.

"Lockdown! Locks, Lights, Out of Sight!
Lockdown! Locks, Lights, Out of Sight!"

ACTIONS

The Lockdown Action demands locking individual classroom doors, offices and other securable areas, moving occupants out of the line of sight of corridor windows, turning off lights to make the room seem unoccupied, and having occupants maintain silence.

There is no call to action to lock the building's exterior access points. Rather, the protocol advises leaving the perimeter as is. The reasoning is simple - sending staff to lock outside doors exposes them to unnecessary risk and inhibits first responders' entry into the building. If the exterior doors are already locked, leave them locked but do have a conversation with your local responders so they understand and can gain access during a Lockdown. The best option is to have the ability to lock and unlock doors remotely.

Training reinforces the practice of not opening the classroom door once in Lockdown. No indication of occupancy should be revealed until first responders open the door.

If the location of the threat is apparent and people do not have the option to get behind a door, it is appropriate to self-evacuate away from the threat.

INCIDENT COMMAND SYSTEM

The School Incident Command System should be initiated.

RESPONSIBILITY

The classroom teacher is responsible for implementing their classroom Lockdown. If it is safe to do so, the teacher should gather students into the classroom prior to locking the door. The teacher should lock all classroom access points and facilitate moving occupants out of sight.

REPORTED BY

When there is a life safety threat on campus, a Lockdown should be immediately initiated by any student or staff member. Initiating the Lockdown may happen through various methods, or a combination of methods, depending on the procedures and alert systems utilized by each school and district. Lockdown alerts may be made by word of mouth, phone, radio systems, intercom, panic buttons, or more advanced forms of technology. Plan the communication method in advance to set expectations for students and staff. Regardless of the method(s) of notification, the initiation of a Lockdown should be consistent, simple and swift, and include immediate notification of school administration and local law enforcement agencies.

PREPARATION

Identification of classroom access points that must be locked in the event of a Lockdown is essential preparation. These may include doorways, windows, loading docks, and fire escape ladder access points.

A "safe zone" should also be identified within the classroom that is out of sight of interior windows. Teachers and students should be trained to not open the classroom door, leaving a first responder, school safety team member or school administrator to unlock it.

DRILLS

Lockdown drills should be performed at least twice a year, or as mandated by state requirements. If possible one of these drills should be performed with local law enforcement personnel participation. At a minimum, law enforcement participation in the drill should occur no less than once every two years.

A drill should always be announced as a drill.

For more information, see the *"SRP Lockdown Drill"* section of this book.

LOCKDOWN
Locks, Lights, Out of Sight

CONTINGENCIES

Students and staff who are outside of classrooms when a Lockdown is announced should try to get into the closest available classroom, or room with a door that can be secured. In the event someone cannot get into a room before doors are locked, they should be instructed about other options. In this situation, students and staff should be trained to hide or even evacuate themselves away from the building or area. Students and staff should receive training on where to go if they self-evacuate so they can be safe and accounted for.

If during a Lockdown an additional hazard manifests inside the school such as a fire, flood, or hazmat incident, then situational decisions must be made. There should be discussions about reacting to a fire alarm if it is activated during a Lockdown. This may require following additional directives of the SRP.

EXAMPLES OF LOCKDOWN CONDITIONS

The following are a few examples of when a school or emergency dispatch might call for a Lockdown.

- Dangerous animal within a school building
- Intruder
- An angry or violent parent or student
- Report of a weapon
- Active assailant

THE DURATION OF A LOCKDOWN

A question that occasionally arises is "How long does it take to release a Lockdown?" The answer is, "That depends, but probably longer than you want to hear."

The Foundation has heard accounts of a Lockdown lasting for hours. In one case - a weapon report - the school was in Lockdown for over three hours. In another - an active assailant in the building - it took about an hour after the issue was resolved for law enforcement to clear the classrooms.

RED CARD/GREEN CARD

Red Card/Green Cards should NOT be used for a Lockdown. Based on a number of tactical assessments, the overwhelming consensus is that this practice provides information to an intruder that there are potential targets in that room.

CELL PHONES DURING A LOCKDOWN

It is not uncommon for school administrators to ban cell phone use during a Lockdown. Parent instincts may be at odds with that ban. Often, one of the first things a parent will do when there is a crisis in the school is text or call their child.

In evaluating actual Lockdown events, the initial crisis may only take minutes. After the threat is mitigated, Law Enforcement typically clears the school one classroom at a time. This process may take significant time. During this time, both parents and students can reduce stress through text communications. This also provides a classroom management strategy. Selecting three or four students at a time, a teacher may ask students to text their parents with a message like this: "We're in Lockdown. I'm okay and I'll update you every 5 minutes." Certainly, if a threat is imminent, texting would be discouraged.

There is also an opportunity to ask the students to text their parents with crafted messages as an event unfolds. For example, "Pick me up at Lincoln Elementary in one hour. Bring your ID," might be recommended for student-parent reunification.

It may also be beneficial to have students turn off both Wi-Fi and cellular data services in order to free up bandwidth for first responders, while still allowing SMS text messaging.

EVACUATION

If an actual violent incident occurred, expect that the building will be evacuated by Law Enforcement since it has become a crime scene.

SRP K12 2023 | Version 4.1 | 06/15/2022

LOCKDOWN
Locks, Lights, Out of Sight

SAMPLE OUTWARD MESSAGING TO PARENTS

This is a guide for outward messaging when a Lockdown Action is used in the school. Because a Lockdown is stressful for everyone, plan to send multiple messages. Have a central digital platform that your public information team can easily update, and people can go to for information.

If a Lockdown will be followed by an off-site evacuation, get that information out as quickly as possible. include the information here, or in a separate communication thread.

Current Lockdown

Email

Subject Line: Safety Notification - Lockdown Currently Activated at *[School Name]*

Dear Parent or Guardian,

[School Name] is currently in Lockdown due to *[state the facts you know about the situation]*.

The safety and security of your child is our top priority. We are actively responding to the situation and collaborating with emergency responders.

At this time, we ask that parents stay where they are and remain available to receive updates and instructions as needed.

Watch for updates here *[link to the platform you'll be updating]*

What is a Lockdown?*

Text Message:

[School Name] is currently in Lockdown. Check your email or voicemail for more information. Please stay where you are and remain available at this time. Look here *[link to social media page/site]* for updates.

Phone Call

Parents, *[School Name]* is currently in Lockdown due to *[state the facts you know about the situation]*. At this time, we ask that parents stay where they are and remain available to receive updates and instructions as needed. Check our *[social media page/site]* for ongoing updates.

Lifted Lockdown

Email

Subject Line: Safety Notification - Lockdown Ended at *[School Name]*

Dear Parent or Guardian,

[School Name] was placed in Lockdown from *[start time of Lockdown]* to *[end time of Lockdown]* due to *[state the incident that occurred]*.

Thank you for your patience while we worked with first responders to respond to the situation.

The safety and security of your child is our top priority.

What is a Lockdown? *

Text Message

The Lockdown at *[School Name]* has been lifted. Please check your email or voicemail for more information.

Phone Call

Parents, the Lockdown at *[School Name]* has been lifted. The school was in Lockdown from *[state Lockdown start time]* to *[state Lockdown end time]* due to *[state the incident that occurred]*. Thank you for your patience while we worked with first responders to respond to the situation.

---

* Lockdown is called when there is a threat or hazard inside the school building. The Lockdown Action demands locking interior doors, moving occupants out of the line of sight of corridor windows, turning off lights to make the room seem unoccupied, and having occupants maintain silence. If students are unable to get behind a locked door, they are trained to self-evacuate. If your child contacts you to let you know that they safely self-evacuated, please contact the district at *[District Phone Number or Safety Hotline]* to notify us your child is safe.

Link to either your website or iloveuguys.org/The-Standard-Response-Protocol.html for them to learn more.

EVACUATE
A Location may also be provided

EVACUATE TO A LOCATION

Evacuate is called when there is a need to move people from one location to another for safety reasons.

An on-site evacuation is conducted usually because of a mechanical failure that would disrupt the school day, such as a power outage. If it can't be resolved quickly, the school may have to plan for early dismissal.

An offsite evacuation may be necessary when it's no longer safe to stay in the building such as a gas leak or bomb threat. In this case, people will be allowed to bring their personal items with them.

If there has been a violent event at the school, an off-site evacuation will almost always be necessary since the school will be deemed a crime scene. People may or may not be able to bring their personal items with them.

REUNIFICATION AFTER AN EVACUATION

When the students and staff are evacuated off-site, they may be walking to a different location or being transported to the location and there will be an organized reunification of students and parents/guardians at that site.

For in-depth information about conducting a Reunification, please refer to The Standard Reunification Method: https://iloveuguys.org/The-Standard-Reunification-Method.html

PUBLIC ADDRESS

The public address for Evacuate is: "Evacuate! To a Location" and is repeated twice each time the public address is performed. For instance, "Evacuate! To the Flag Pole."

"Evacuate! To a location.
Evacuate! To a location."

ACTIONS

The Evacuate Action demands students and staff move in an orderly fashion to a safe area.

INCIDENT COMMAND SYSTEM

The School Incident Command System should be initiated.

RESPONSIBILITY

The classroom teacher or administrator is usually responsible for initiating an Evacuation. The directives or actions may vary for fire, bomb threat, or other emergencies. Other directions may be invoked during an evacuation, and students and staff should be prepared to follow specific instructions given by staff or first responders.

PREPARATION

Evacuation preparation involves the identification of facility evacuation routes, evacuation assembly points and evacuation sites, as well as student, teacher, and administrator training. An evacuation site usually becomes the reunification site, so plan accordingly. Ideally, plan to have an offsite evacuation facility that's within walking distance and another father away from the school in case the hazard is in the immediate area. Have an MOU in place with each site to outline expectations and responsibilities in advance. A sample MOU for this can be downloaded from iloveuguys.org/The-Standard-Response-Protocol.html

An Evacuation plan must include having all supplies that people with disabilities may need such as medications, supplementary mobility devices and accessible routes for mobility-impaired people.

EVACUATION ASSEMBLY

The Evacuation Assembly refers to gathering at the Evacuation Assembly Point(s). Teachers are instructed to take roll after arrival at the Evacuation Assembly Point(s).

Schools with large populations might plan on having multiple, predetermined assembly points to help manage crowds.

DRILLS

Evacuation drills should be performed at least twice a year or as mandated by state law. An Evacuation drill is very similar to a fire drill. Fire drills are often required regularly and constitute a valid Evacuation drill.

Drills are also a good opportunity to talk about and practice alternate exit routes to use in case a certain area is not safe to walk through.

CONTINGENCIES

Students are trained that if they are separated from their class during an Evacuation, then joining another group is acceptable. They should be instructed to identify themselves to the teacher in their group after arriving at the Evacuation Site.

RED CARD/GREEN CARD/MED CARD

After taking roll, the Red/Green/Med Card system is employed for administrators or first responders to quickly visually identify the status of the teachers' classes. Teachers will hold up the Green card if they have all their students and are good to go. They hold up the Red card if they are missing students, have extra students or another problem, and use the Med card to indicate their need for some sort of medical attention.

See the Materials section for examples.

SRP K12 2023 | Version 4.1 | 06/15/2022

SAMPLE OUTWARD MESSAGING TO PARENTS

This is a guide for outward messaging when an Evacuation is necessary. Evacuations can be stressful because they are disruptive, whether they're on-site or off-site, so plan to send multiple messages. Have a central digital platform that your public information team can easily update, and people can go to for information.

Variables in the message are in italic type.

Evacuation with a return to school anticipated

Email

Subject Line: Safety Notification - *[School Name]* Has Been Evacuated

Dear Parent or Guardian,

[School Name] was Evacuated at *[state evacuation time]* due to *[state reason for evacuation]*.

The safety and security of your child is our top priority. We are actively responding to the situation and collaborating with emergency responders.

The *[state the reason for evacuation]* is expected to be resolved with students returning to class. Dismissal will be at the regular time today. Watch for updates here *[link to the platform you'll be updating]*

What is the Evacuate Action? *

Text Message

[School Name] has been Evacuated due to *[state reason for evacuation]*. Please check your email and voicemail for details and information.

Phone Call

Parents, *[School Name]* has been Evacuated due to *[state reason for evacuation]*. Please check your email for details and information.

Evacuation with early dismissal planned

Email

Subject Line: Safety Notification - *[School Name]* Has Been Evacuated

Dear Parent or Guardian,

[School Name] was Evacuated at *[state evacuation time]* due to *[state reason for evacuation]*. Because of *[reason]*, there will be an early dismissal at *[state the time]*.

The safety and security of your child is our top priority. We are actively responding to the situation and collaborating with emergency responders. Watch for updates here *[link to the platform you'll be updating]*

What is the Evacuate Action? *

Text Message

[School Name] has been Evacuated due to *[state reason for evacuation]* and students will be dismissed early at *[state the time]*. Please check your email and voicemail for details.

Phone Call

Parents, *[School Name]* has been Evacuated due to *[state reason for evacuation]* and students will be dismissed early at *[state the time]*. Please check your email for details and information.

Evacuation to an off-site location

Email

Subject Line: Safety Notification - *[School Name]* Has Been Evacuated

Dear Parent or Guardian,

[School Name] was Evacuated at *[state evacuation time]* due to *[state reason for evacuation]*.

The safety and security of your child is our top priority. We are actively responding to the situation and collaborating with emergency responders.

At this time, we ask that parents stay where they are and remain available to receive updates and instructions as needed.

You will receive communications as soon as we have additional details and information on when and where to pick your child up. Please bring your ID and your patience when you are picking up your child.

Watch for updates here *[link to the platform you'll be updating]*

What is the Evacuate Action? *

Text Message

[School Name] has been Evacuated due to *[state reason for evacuation]* which renders the building unsafe at this time. Students can be picked up at *[alternate location]* after *[time]*. Please check your email and voicemail for details. Please bring your ID and your patience when you are picking up your child.

Phone Call

Parents, *[School Name]* was Evacuated at *[state evacuation time]* due to *[state reason for evacuation]*. At this time, we ask that parents stay where they are and remain available to receive updates and instructions as needed. We will update you with further communications as soon as we have additional details and information on when and where to pick your child up. Please check your email for details and information.

---

* Evacuate is called when there is a need to move people from one location to another. During an evacuation, students and staff are asked to move from one location to another in an orderly fashion.

Link to either your website or iloveuguys.org/The-Standard-Response-Protocol.html for them to learn more.

POLICE LED
Evacuation after a Lockdown

POLICE LED EVACUATION
In the rare situations where law enforcement is clearing classrooms and escorting students and staff out of the classroom and through the building, it is important to have provided advance instruction on what to expect.

PUBLIC ADDRESS
There may or may not be any public address notifying students and staff that law enforcement is performing these actions.

ACTIONS
As officers enter the classroom, students and staff must keep their hands visible and empty. It is unlikely they will be able to bring backpacks, purses or any personal items with them during a Police Led Evacuation. Students may be instructed to form a single file line and hold hands front and back, or students and staff may be asked to put their hands on their heads while evacuating.

WHAT TO EXPECT
Prepare students and staff that during a Police Led Evacuation, officers may be loud, direct and commanding. Students and staff may also be searched both in the classroom and again after exiting the building.

EMOTIONAL RESPONSIBILITY
There is a conversation occurring with law enforcement regarding their role in post-event recovery. This is a growing concern, and warrants conversations between schools, districts, and agencies about how to keep students safe, and reduce trauma that might be associated with a Police Led Evacuation.

PREPARATION
Student, teacher, and administrator training.

In the event of a police led evacuation, policies should be in place on how to give key access to law enforcement officers evacuating all rooms in the school building.

MEDIA MESSAGING
To the media/community after an event.

Example Situation: Violent Event

"On (date) at (time of day), (agency name) responded to (school name) in reference to (event type). Officers assisted with safely escorting students and staff out of the school and to the Evacuation and Reunification site where the (School District) was able to initiate the Reunification process."

DISPATCH MESSAGING
To responding officers during an event.

Example Situation: Police Led Evacuation

"(*Dispatched Units*) respond to (*school name*) to assist with Evacuation of students and staff. Assistance is needed to accompany individuals out of the school and to the Secure Assembly Area at (*location*). Respond to the Command Post for your assignment. (*time stamp*)"

LAW ENFORCEMENT MESSAGING
To responding officers during an event.

Example Situation: Gas Leak

(*Police unit name*) respond to (*area near the school*) to assist with evacuating students from (*school name*) because of a gas smell in the building. Meet with (*supervisor*) for further information to assist with Evacuation and Reunification.

LAW ENFORCEMENT GUIDANCE
Once the threat has been neutralized, it is recommended that first responders re-group and slowly move to the evacuation phase. Identify the location of the evacuation area or bus staging area prior to releasing classrooms. Take this time to discuss emotional responsibility when releasing classrooms. Begin releasing people from classrooms and offices to the designated area.

Law enforcement officers may also be needed to assist with directing traffic and ensuring the evacuation process is being done safely.

CONTINGENCIES
In an off-site evacuation to a reunification site, Incident Commanders should consider leaving students and staff in their rooms until transportation arrives. Your team can also discuss communicating to classrooms that the threat has been minimized enough that they may relax and wait for evacuation.

When it's time, each room can be cleared directly to the buses in order to minimize trauma.

It is recommended to avoid the scene of the incident when exiting. Transport directly to the Reunification Site.

TRANSPORTATION
During a police led evacuation, transportation is going to be initiated. Have a policy in place for your transportation department or contracted transportation company so they are ready to respond in a timely manner with enough buses.

SHELTER
State the Hazard and Safety Strategy

SHELTER
STATE THE HAZARD AND SAFETY STRATEGY

Shelter is called when specific protective actions are needed based on a threat or hazard. Training should include response to threats such as tornadoes, earthquakes, hazardous materials situations or other local threats.

PUBLIC ADDRESS

The public address for Shelter should include the hazard and the safety strategy. The public address is repeated twice each time the public address is performed.

"Shelter! For a hazard. Using safety strategy.
Shelter! For a hazard. Using safety strategy."

For a tornado, an example would be:

"Shelter for a tornado. Go to the tornado shelter.
Shelter for a tornado. Go to the tornado shelter."

After the danger has passed:

"Students and staff, the Shelter is released. All clear.

Thank you for your assistance and patience during the Shelter."

HAZARDS MAY INCLUDE
- Tornado
- Severe weather
- Wildfires
- Flooding
- Hazmat spill or release
- Earthquake
- Tsunami

SAFETY STRATEGIES MAY INCLUDE
- Evacuate to Shelter area
- Seal the room
- Drop, cover and hold
- Get to high ground

ACTIONS

Collaboration with local responders, the National Weather Service, and other local, regional and state resources will help in developing specific actions for your district response.

INCIDENT COMMAND SYSTEM

The School Incident Command System should be initiated.

RESPONSIBILITY

Sheltering requires that all students and staff follow response directives. Districts should have procedures for all foreseeable local hazards and threats which include provisions for those individuals with access and functional needs.

PREPARATION

Identification and marking of facility Shelter areas.

DRILLS

Shelter safety strategies should be drilled at least twice a year, or as mandated by the state.

STATE THE HAZARD AND SAFETY STRATEGY

Using the Shelter Protocol and stating the hazard allows for an understanding of the threat and the associated protective actions. Most often, the Shelter Protocol is utilized for tornadoes and other severe weather, in which case it would include the Shelter location for students and staff, and what protective posture or action they should take.

Sheltering for a hazardous materials spill or release is very different. In the case of a hazmat situation, students and staff would be directed to close their windows, shut down their heating and air conditioning units and seal windows and doors to preserve the good inside air while restricting the entry of any contaminated outside air. Listening to specific directives is critical to successful emergency response.

PLAIN LANGUAGE

NIMS and ICS require the use of plain language. Codes and specific language that are not readily understood by the general public are no longer to be used. The SRP uses shared, plain, natural language between students, staff and first responders. If there are specific directives that need to be issued for a successful response in a school, those should be made clearly using plain language. There is nothing wrong with adding directives as to where to Shelter, or what protective actions should be used in the response.

CUSTOMIZATION

The classroom poster is sufficient for generic Shelter guidance. The Foundation recognizes that localized hazards may need to be added to the poster. For this reason, the Public Address poster is available in MS Word for customization (https://iloveuguys.org/The-Standard-Response-Protocol.html).

SHELTER
State the Hazard and Safety Strategy

SAMPLE OUTWARD MESSAGING TO PARENTS

This is a guide for outward messaging when a Shelter Action is necessary. In a weather event, which is a commonly the reason this is used, it's likely that families are also sheltering. They will want to know their children are in a safe situation. Have a central digital platform that your public information team can easily update, and people can go to for information.

Shelter (Current)

Email

Subject Line: Safety Notification - Shelter Currently Activated at [School Name]

Dear Parent or Guardian,

[School Name] is currently Sheltering due to [state reason for Shelter].

The safety and security of your child is our top priority. We are actively monitoring the situation.

Watch for updates here [link to the platform you'll be updating]

What is Shelter? *

Text Message

[School Name] is currently Sheltering due to [state reason for Shelter]. Please check your email and voicemail for more information.

Phone Call

Parents, [School Name] is currently Sheltering due to [state reason for Shelter]. The safety and security of your child is our top priority. Please check your email for more information. We are actively monitoring the situation and will send updates as necessary.

Shelter (Past)

Email

Subject Line: Safety Notification - Shelter Ended at [School Name]

Dear Parent or Guardian,

[School Name] used the Shelter Action from [start time of Shelter] to [end time of Shelter] due to [state reason for Shelter]. All school operations have now returned to normal.

The safety and security of your child is our top priority. We will continue to keep you informed about important concerns at our school.

Watch for updates here [link to the platform you'll be updating]

What is Shelter? *

Shelter is called when specific protective actions are needed based on a threat or hazard. Sheltering requires that all students and staff follow response directives based on the threat or hazard.

Link to either your website or *iloveuguys.org/The-Standard-Response-Protocol.html* for them to learn more. protocol at iloveuguys.org/The-Standard-Response-Protocol.html

Text Message

The Shelter at [School Name] has been lifted. All school operations have now returned to normal.

Please check your email and voicemail for more information.

Phone Call

[School Name] used the Shelter Action from [start time of Shelter] to [end time of Shelter] due to [state reason for Shelter]. All school operations have now returned to normal.

* Shelter is called when specific protective actions are needed based on a threat or hazard. Sheltering requires that all students and staff follow response directives based on the threat or hazard.

Link to either your website or *iloveuguys.org/The-Standard-Response-Protocol.html* for them to learn more.

SRP K12 2023 | Version 4.1 | 06/15/2022

SEQUENCING
The Actions

HOLD **SECURE** **LOCKDOWN** **EVACUATE** **SHELTER**

The five actions of the Standard Response Protocol can work together as situations evolve and information is gathered. Here are some examples of how this can, and has, been done.

HOLD ESCALATES TO LOCKDOWN

The school receives a vague or anonymous report, through social media, of a student carrying a weapon. There is neither an immediate confirmation of it nor a substantiated threat. School personnel needs time to locate the student and send security/SRO to locate and confront the student in a very low-key way. They initiate the Hold Action during the search. Additional information and evidence may lead to a Lockdown because an imminent threat is detected.

LOCKDOWN MISTAKE SHIFTS TO SECURE

The Police Department received reports from passers-by of a person with a rifle on the bike path adjacent to an elementary school. They called the school directly and directed them to put the school in Lockdown, which was incorrect but this can happen when there are many unknown factors. Officers and District Security Teams were on the scene within 2-5 minutes and a suspect was taken into custody within that time. Personnel on-site were able to quickly confirm the building wasn't breached.

The Lockdown was shifted to a Secure Action, with each classroom being released by school and security personnel. Releasing each classroom instead of using a public address is to retain continuity for releasing any Lockdown.

SECURE ESCALATES TO LOCKDOWN

Recently there was a shooting in a park adjacent to a high school. The school was immediately placed in Secure, however, several victims and witness students ran back inside before the doors could be secured. In this case, it was unknown exactly who entered the building. The Secure Action shifted to Lockdown as a precaution while officers searched the building. It was determined to be safe within about 30 minutes, but the Lockdown was not immediately lifted. Moving to Hold at that point may have been a better choice in order to manage the situation and maintain tactical control of the building while allowing some monitored movement inside.

HOLD TO EVACUATE

Utilize a Hold Action for a brief time during an unexpected fire alarm that is not accompanied by immediate signs of smoke or fire. This allows safety/security teams to scan for actual signs of fire, or other ambush type threats before Evacuating the building. An Evacuation would still occur per fire department requirements, but the tactical pause to gather information before evacuating allows for more situational awareness.

ENVIRONMENT
Dictates the Tactics

WHERE YOU ARE DICTATES WHAT YOU DO

The SRP was designed as an all-hazards model for incident response. The protocol is easily modifiable for any location or environment. It is not necessary to list every possible scenario that may occur, as the protocol provides universal response actions. A school's action in response to a fire is an evacuation. To prepare for this evacuation drills are practiced, not fire drills. This is the same response that would occur due to a gas leak, or long-term power outage in winter conditions. By preparing for and practicing evacuation drills the school is prepared for any eventuality that may require the staff and students to leave the school location.

Your specific environment will dictate what additional plans or resources you may need. For example, a school in Alaska must think about warming locations for winter evacuations while a school in Arizona will need to think about cooling areas for a summer evacuation.

GLASS. LOTS OF GLASS

Glass is always one of the weakest points of building security. As more and more schools are built with the open concept, we are seeing walls of glass throughout buildings. While beneficial for increased light and a sense of openness, they provide little protection. If your school has interior glass walls or large interior windows we recommend you plan to purchase window film and some sort of shade system. The film will increase the strength of the glass and the shades will offer concealment.

Similar steps should be taken on the perimeter of buildings. Main entrances traditionally have large glass doors. Film is appropriate here as well. Be sure to inspect your school and note areas of potential weakness and address them appropriately.

DISTRIBUTED CAMPUS

Some school locations have a distributed campus with multiple buildings spread out over the property, similar to a college environment. The layout of a distributed campus brings unique challenges for school and district staff. Your jurisdictions will need to develop specific policies for each action. Additionally, it will be crucial for staff to be expertly trained on the process so they can use their judgment when needed. Nearly every action will have variations that may be necessary for a distributed environment.

Both Hold and Secure can be applied to the entire school property or only to specific buildings as appropriate. Whoever enacts the protocols will need to provide enough details for proper decisions to be made. If exact details are unknown then it is best to treat each building as an individual school and place the entire property into the protocol until more information is known.

During the Secure Action, there is some type of threat outside the school building. The action is for everyone to move inside, lock outside doors, and continue the day as usual. In a distributed campus more information about the threat is going to be needed.

If the threat is on school property, such as a dangerous animal roaming the grounds, then each building should go into Secure with students remaining where they are.

If the threat is off the property and a perimeter can be established then it may be appropriate for movement between buildings to occur but no one on or off the school property. An alternative approach could be to have security or law enforcement escort students and staff between buildings. The exact situation and your school's specific layout will determine your actions.

If the exact location of the threat is unknown, then it is better to err on the side of caution and keep everyone within their respective buildings.

A Hold will need to be handled similarly. If the reason for a Hold only affects a single building then it may be appropriate for only that building to go into the Hold protocol. However, you will need to make sure no students or staff are leaving other buildings and entering the Hold area.

TEMPORARY OR MODULAR BUILDINGS OR CLASSROOMS

Additional policy will be needed if your school has temporary or modular buildings. One option is to treat them in the same way as a distributed campus. Alternatively, if it is appropriate, and depending on the size of the school, students and staff from these areas can be brought into the main building.

SRP K12 2023 | Version 4.1 | 06/15/2022

MATERIALS
And a Note for your Printer

NOTE TO PRINTERS

All materials are available to download from https://iloveuguys.org/The-Standard-Response-Protocol.html

This material may be duplicated for distribution per "SRP Terms of Use," which reads as follows:

Terms of Use: District/school is responsible for physical material production of any online resources provided by The Foundation. The District/school is not required to utilize printing services provided by The Foundation for production of support materials.

What this means: You may have print these yourself or send them to a printer.

Terms of Use: School District agrees to incorporate the SRP using the terms of art and the associated directives as defined in the Program Description.

What this means: The school, district, agency or organization may place their logo and/or name on printed material to personalize it. They may not substantively change the wording or actions, except as it applies to hazards specific to their region.

PRINTING THE BOOKS

Books have been laid out with a 5 pica (.83") interior margin and a 4 pica (.67") exterior margin to facilitate duplex printing of the materials. Books can be finished using common bindery methods: perfect bind, comb bind, spiral bind, saddle stitch, or punch for a 3-ring binder.

SRP CLASSROOM POSTER

This K12 SRP overview wall poster was created to be printed and placed on walls in order to remind everyone of the different SRP actions and allow teachers to start the conversation about SRP with their students.

Placing posters is an essential step in the full implementation of the SRP. The poster should be displayed in every classroom, near building entries, and at the entrances to the cafeteria, auditorium and gym. The Shelter hazards and safety strategies can be modified for local conditions.

The poster is available in letter size (8.5 x 11") and tabloid size (11 x 17"), in English and Spanish.

PUBLIC ADDRESS PROTOCOL POSTER

The Public Address Protocol Poster can be placed near all reasonable public address locations. This is a sample. Your district, department or agency should customize this poster for regional hazards. It is available to download in Microsoft Word format. The public address is repeated twice each time the public address is performed.

Hold! In your room or area. Clear the halls.

Secure! Get Inside. Lock outside doors.

Lockdown! Locks, Lights, Out of Sight.

Evacuate! To a Location.

Shelter! State the Hazard and Safety Strategy.

INFORMATION FOR PARENTS AND GUARDIANS

Clear communication to parents and guardians about the SRP is essential so they understand the actions your school will be using. By being as clear as possible, you can reduce the amount of stress they might experience for even the small disruptions in a school day.

They need to understand their roles in any incident. The letter-size handout is in PDF format and can be emailed or printed to hand out. It describes what is expected of people in the school, and outlines the roles of the parents and guardians during Secure and Lockdown events.

Schools should outline the methods with which they will be communicating with parents and guardians about any drill or actual incident. It is imperative that parents and guardians keep their contact information up to date with the school and district.

Additionally, there is a web page for parents to go to for detailed information and conversations. Your school or district is welcome to post this on your website for easy access.

The Parent Handout is available in accessible PDF formats in English and Spanish.

MATERIALS
And a Note for your Printer

STATUS POSTERS

Letter-size posters for use to communicate the status of the school during drills or incidents.

These include posters for two levels of Secure conditions, and a Lockdown Drill Poster.

VIDEO TRAINING

There are some videos you can download from http://iloveuguys.org, or YouTube, to use for training purposes.

The Standard Response Protocol (SRP) for Students (7:26)

This is a teenage student speaking with a School Resource Officer about the actions of the SRP. It's appropriate for students in middle school and older.

Lockdown Drill with Standard Response Protocol (3:35)

This was recorded during a High School Lockdown drill. It includes interviews with students, and is appropriate for all ages of students.

For the Little Ones

There are links on the website to training modules that were created for younger students by school districts. We link to those with permission by the creators.

ID CARDS

Art for printing onto identification cards is available for slotted and unslotted cards in the standard size of 3.375" x 2.125".

POCKET GUIDE

This is a quick guide to the five actions. It folds to the size of a business card to fit in wallets, pockets, and ID cardholders. It prints on two sides of letter-size paper and there are three to a page.

RED CARD/GREEN CARD

This is for use in an Evacuation Assembly to do a quick assessment of the status of all groups. It is not for classroom use during a Lockdown or Lockdown Drill.

There are three different types for different situations, so choose to use the one that's best for your environment.

After arriving at an Evacuation Assembly and taking roll, the Red/Green Cards are used for administration or first responders to quickly and visually identify the status of the teachers' classes after an evacuation.

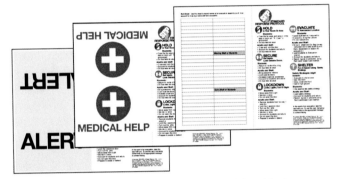

Green Card (OK) - All students accounted for, No immediate help is necessary

Red Card (Help) - Extra or missing students, or vital information must be exchanged

Red/GREEN/Med Card

Red and White Cross (Medical Help) - Immediate medical attention is needed

Red/GREEN/Roll Card

This includes a roll sheet for users to record who is in their group.

Red/GREEN/Alert Card

The Alert card is used to indicate there is a problem in your group and you need assistance.

DRILLS
vs. Functional & Full-Scale Exercises

Here are some definitions and descriptions of drills and exercises. This is a compilation from various sources and includes the important points from each one. It includes information gained by experience with actual drills and exercises in schools and districts.

DRILLS VS. EXERCISES

Media coverage exploring issues with lockdown drills potentially causing trauma has resulted in the need for clarification. Much of the coverage attributed the word "Drill" to what was actually a "Drill Game or Functional Exercise."

School lockdown drills are not synonymous with functional exercises. Nor are they understood and practiced properly. According to FEMA (see Appendix A), exercises help build preparedness by allowing organizations to test and validate plans, determine strengths, and identify areas for improvement.

SCENARIO, OR NO SCENARIO

It is important to note that any type of exercise can be conducted with or without a scenario. The I Love U Guys Foundation recommends an all-hazards approach to exercise design and development, where the main goal is to practice or test a specific capability. For example, a functional exercise could be designed to practice inter-agency coordination in response to a large-scale power outage. The reason for the outage does not matter. At times a scenario can enhance the realism of an exercise but it is not needed.

The I Love U Guys Foundation uses this approach during reunification exercises and it is also recommended for Evacuation, Lockdown, Secure, and Hold drills.

DRILL

The primary objective of a drill is for participants to build muscle memory, and practice an action to use in various events or situations. A secondary objective is for the people who are administering the drill to validate procedures, clarify roles and identify operational process gaps.

Drills are for staff and students, and are educational opportunities to practice life safety skills. For example, an evacuation drill is conducted at schools worldwide regularly. A fire alarm goes off, students line up and head outside. There is no trauma in these events because there is no simulation of a threat or hazard. Schools do not light fires in the hallways to simulate an evacuation due to fire.

Lockdown drills are similar. There is no simulated violence needed to conduct them. The only information needed is for the protocol to be enacted, "Lockdown, locks, lights, out of sight," and then students and staff perform the proper functions.

EXERCISE - TWO CATEGORIES

There are several types of exercises, which are divided into two categories. The categories are discussion-based exercises and operations-based exercises.

Discussion-based exercises are designed to introduce concepts to organizations. They allow individuals to become familiar with policies and procedures. Seminars, workshops, tabletops, and games are types of discussion-based exercises. Some of those will include talking about scenarios and regional hazards, and what sort of response might be required for those specific issues.

Operations-based exercises involve actual response actions and are used to practice or validate plans and policies. The learning objective is to test response, capacity, and resources across the system. Students are rarely asked to engage with these. An exercise can include a description or enactment of an incident, but doesn't have to.

Exercises are broader in scope than drills, and are designed to encourage people to think on their toes, work together, and apply lessons learned from drills.

Invite people from your community to participate as volunteers in an exercise, or to observe it. You will probably be introducing scenarios they have thought about, and this level of engagement can be useful.

In a Functional Exercise, participants perform their duties in a simulated environment. Functional exercises typically focus on specific team members and/or procedures and are often used to identify process gaps associated with multi-agency coordination, command and control.

The "I Love U Guys" Foundation's reunification exercises (Rex) are an example of a functional exercise. During these, participants test and practice the capabilities of the reunification team to properly reunite students with the appropriate parent or guardian. The exercise starts with notification that students were evacuated from the school and are already at the reunification site.

A Full-Scale exercise is similar in execution to a Functional exercise and is as close to the real thing as possible. It can include employees from multiple functions, community first responders, local businesses, and regulatory agencies. This type of exercise should utilize, to the extent possible, the actual systems and equipment that would be dispatched during a real incident. From a duration standpoint, full-scale exercises often take place over the course of an entire business day.

SRP EVOLUTION
In developing the Standard Response Protocol, The "I Love U Guys" Foundation took the following approach:

* Identify the hazard;
* Develop response;
* Train;
* Practice;
* Drill;
* Exercise.

PROBLEM IDENTIFICATION
The first priority of the SRP was to introduce common, plain language responses to various events. An assessment of various school responses in 2009 revealed there was no common language between students, staff, parents, media, and first responders. The core areas examined were:

* Something happening outside the school;
* Something is happening inside of the school;
* How to get out of the school;
* Natural or man-made hazards;
* Keeping the halls clear.

DEVELOP RESPONSE
Given those conditions, the Standard Response Protocol was developed, piloted and released.

TRAIN
The next step in the process is providing training to students and staff on each of the response protocols, which can be done with the downloadable materials.

PRACTICE
Once training has been delivered, practice is recommended prior to any drill. This may initially involve a discussion between staff and students to:

* Find various exit routes in advance of an Evacuation drill;
* Discuss ways to protect oneself from various weather hazards prior to a Shelter drill;
* Identify Safe Zones within a classroom and practice moving students to those zones prior to a Lockdown drill;
* Talk about situations that may require a Secure or Hold action.

COMMUNICATING ABOUT DRILLS
Prior to conducting any drills, schools are advised to send concise communication to parents and guardians about the nature and objectives of, and reason for, the drill. This can be done with an email or letter or both. It is not necessary to state the exact day or time of certain drills.

If parents feel their student(s) will be upset by certain drills, invite them to attend, or give them a chance to opt their family out of the drill. If possible, arrange to have an opt-out student stay on school grounds, but not participate, in order to minimize disruption to the school day.

LOCKDOWN DRILL GUIDANCE
A critical aspect in implementing the SRP with fidelity is the Lockdown Drill. Successful drills provide participants with the "muscle memory" should an actual Lockdown occur. Drills also reveal deficiencies that may exist in either procedures, training or personnel.

Understand that a Lockdown drill is for practicing an action, not an event. An actual Lockdown can occur due to a variety of threatening situations which may present an immediate and ongoing danger to the safety of students, staff and visitors within a building.

PREPARATION
Prior to drilling, students, staff and administration should review the SRP Training Presentation, which is available on https://iloveuguys.org/The-Standard-Response-Protocol.html. Administration should also verify with law enforcement their use of the SRP in the school or district.

Teachers should take time with students to identify and occupy a "Safe Zone" in the classroom where they cannot be seen through any corridor windows. If visibility in a classroom is problematic, window coverings or alternative locations should be identified. Speak with local law enforcement about their preference for using window coverings.

Additionally, the following instructions should be delivered to students.

* Locate yourself at a point in the classroom where you can no longer see out the corridor window.
* Maintain silence. No cell phone calls.
* Discuss the cell phone policy based on Lockdown guidance on page 22.

PARTNERSHIPS
School-level drills should have district support. There may also be district resources available to assist in conducting the drill. Another key partnership is with local law enforcement. Local patrol, community resource officers or school resource officers should be part of the drill process.

THE EMERGENCY RESPONSE TEAM

Some schools have a pre-identified Building/School Emergency Response Team. These teams are effective for responding to any type of incident.

It is a noted best practice for administration to survey the staff population for prior emergency response, military or law enforcement experience and specialized training and skills for use in district emergency operations.

THE LOCKDOWN DRILL TEAM

During an actual Lockdown, members of the Emergency Response Team may be in classrooms or administrative offices in Lockdown mode and unable to assist with the response.

The Lockdown Drill Team should not include personnel that have specific roles during an actual emergency within that school. Instead, the team might include a school nurse or medical professional, district safety representatives, law enforcement, and those administrators from another school.

STAFF NOTIFICATION

When Lockdown drills are first being introduced to a school, it is absolutely okay to tell staff in advance of the drill. There may be staff members adversely affected by surprise drills.

SPECIAL NEEDS CONSIDERATIONS

It is critical to identify any specific issues that may cause challenges for students with special needs or disabilities and incorporate appropriate actions for notification prior to drills. It is not recommended that additional assistance be provided in special needs areas for drills, UNLESS this assistance is part of the plan and those resources will be assigned in an actual emergency.

THE PRE-DRILL BRIEFING

Prior to the Lockdown drill, a short planning meeting with the Lockdown Drill Team should occur. The agenda is simple:

- Review the floor plan and team member assignments;
- Expected drill duration;
- The door knock and classroom conversation;
- Potential student or staff distress;
- Ensure law enforcement has access to keys to unlock all doors.

ANNOUNCING THE LOCKDOWN DRILL

When using public address to announce a Lockdown drill, repeat, "Lockdown. Locks, Lights, Out of Sight. This is a drill." It's important to tell students and staff that it's a drill. Failure to do so will most likely result in parents, media and maybe even law enforcement coming to the school.

"Lockdown. Locks, Lights, Out of Sight. This is a drill.

Lockdown. Locks, Lights, Out of Sight. This is a drill."

Alternately, consider announcing the drill prior to saying which type of drill it is. This technique will prevent an immediate reaction to the word Lockdown.

"This is a drill. Lockdown. Locks, Lights, Out of Sight"

"This is a drill. Lockdown. Locks, Lights, Out of Sight,"

or

"We are going to conduct a Lockdown drill. Please listen for the Lockdown announcement."

CONDUCTING THE DRILL

The Lockdown Drill Team should be broken into groups of two or three members who go to individual classrooms. One of the members acts as "Scribe" and documents each classroom response. Large schools will need multiple Lockdown Drill Teams in order to complete the drill in a timely fashion.

At the classroom door, team members listen for noise and look through the corridor window for any student or staff visibility or movement. A team member then knocks on the door and requests entry. There should be no response to this request. At this point, a member of the team unlocks the classroom door and announces their name and position. A quick assessment is made by the safety team. The occupants of the room are reminded that they are still in Lockdown and should remain so until they hear an announcement that the drill is completed.

A Lockdown Response Worksheet was created by The "I Love U Guys" Foundation to assist in documenting the Lockdown drills. It can be copied from the following page or downloaded.

WINDOWS

Often there is a conversation about inside and outside windows. Corridor windows are left uncovered so that first responders can see inside the room. Outside windows are left untouched because the threat would be inside the building. There are different preferences regarding window coverings, so please discuss this with your local responders to make sure you're in agreement.

THE CLASSROOM CONVERSATION

Make sure to stake out a few minutes after the room has been checked, and before the release of the drill, to allow for conversation in the classroom.

Typically, this conversation addresses the purpose of the drill, and the observed outcome for that classroom. Additionally, self-evacuation and other life safety strategies can be discussed.

Any issues should be addressed gently but immediately. When possible, have a school counselor available to address any staff or student distress.

THE LOCKDOWN DRILL TEAM DEBRIEF

At the conclusion of the drill, the team should reconvene for a debrief and use this time to review portions of the school safety plan. A good debriefing may reveal some gaps and areas for improvement in the plan.

Any issues should be documented, the safety plan reviewed, and action items identified. An opportunity for all staff to submit information regarding the performance of the drill should be part of the after-action review process.

STANDARD RESPONSE PROTOCOL®

FREQUENTLY ASKED QUESTIONS

Since introducing the Standard Response Protocol in 2009, thousands of districts, departments and agencies have scrutinized, evaluated and ultimately implemented the program. During the process some questions seem to come up often.

SERIOUSLY, WHAT DOES IT REALLY COST?

Since its introduction in 2009, public K12 schools, districts, departments and agencies were free to use The "I Love U Guys" Foundation programs at no cost.

In 2015, the Foundation expanded availability, and now offers the programs to any public or private organization at no charge. Download the materials and begin the process.

WHAT ABOUT BUSINESS/CHURCH/ INSTITUTION USE?

Please look at the materials designed specifically for institutional use on the website. http://iloveuguys.org.

I SEE YOU OFFER TRAINING. DO WE NEED TO BUY TRAINING IN ORDER TO USE THE PROGRAMS?

No. We've attempted to put enough material online so that schools and law enforcement can successfully implement Foundation programs. We know of thousands of schools across the US and Canada that have implemented the programs using internal resources.

That said, part of our sustainability model relies not just on charitable giving, but in providing training for districts ,departments and agencies. If your organization is interested in Foundation training, please contact us for rates and terms.

WHAT IS THE DIFFERENCE BETWEEN SECURE AND LOCKDOWN AGAIN?

The term "Secure" is used when there is a potential threat that can be mitigated by bringing everyone inside. It should be announced with the directive "Get inside. Lock outside doors," which signals to bring people in and lock exterior doors. While it calls for heightened situational awareness, it also allows for indoor activities to continue.

The term "Lockdown" means there is an active or imminent threat inside or nearby requiring immediate protective action. It is followed by the directive "Locks, Lights, Out of Sight" and requires locking classroom doors, turning out the lights, and remaining hidden until first responders arrive.

Effectively if the threat is outside the building, Secure. If the threat is inside the building, Lockdown.

WHAT IF THE THREAT IS CLOSE TO THE BUILDING?

There may be situations where both Secure and Lockdown protocols may be called sequentially. In this case, use Secure to get people inside and lock exterior doors. When the perimeter is Secured, this may become a Lockdown if the threat is persistent and appears to be coming closer. Exterior doors would stay locked.

IN LOCKDOWN, YOU SUGGEST UNLOCKING THE OUTSIDE DOORS. WHAT'S UP WITH THAT?

No, we don't. We occasionally hear this but our guidance is actually a little different. We suggest not putting anyone at risk by locking or unlocking outside doors. If the doors are locked, leave them locked. Be sure you have a plan that allows first responders to enter the building quickly.

WON'T PEOPLE STILL COME IN THE BUILDING IF THE OUTSIDE DOORS ARE UNLOCKED DURING A LOCKDOWN?

Yes, people may be able to enter the building during the window of time between calling a lockdown and the arrival of first responders.

A lockdown is called when there is a life safety threat inside the building. During the development and throughout the lifecycle of the SRP, constant and deliberate scrutiny of all risk/benefit guidance is performed by the Foundation, district and law enforcement representatives. This has resulted in the lockdown guidance provided.

That said, with any guidance provided, we defer to local decisions. If you are a district, please consult with your local law enforcement representatives for final guidance.

I THOUGHT I SAW SHELTER GUIDANCE?

When we developed the SRP and released the first version in 2009 we included FEMA guidance regarding the Shelter directive and actions. FEMA changed that guidance in 2014. We are removing specific shelter guidance from our documentation and defer to the current practices published at http://fema.gov as well as your local emergency management guidance.

CAN THE SRP BE USED IN CONJUNCTION WITH OTHER SAFETY PLANS?

Yes, absolutely. The SRP is designed as an enhancement to any safety plan. It covers critical incidents by standardizing vocabulary so stakeholders can easily understand the status and respond quickly when an unforeseen event occurs. Comprehensive safety plans will include components such as communications, threat assessment, local hazards, operation continuity and reunification, among other items.

CAN I MODIFY MATERIALS?

That depends. The core actions and directives must remain intact. These are:

1. Hold "In your room or area. Clear the halls."

2. Secure "Get inside. Locks outside doors"

3. Lockdown "Locks, Lights, Out of Sight"

4. Evacuate followed by the announced location

5. Shelter followed by the announced hazard and safety strategy

Some details may need to be customized to your location. For instance, the public address poster should be modified to include hazards and safety strategies that are specific to your location.

ARE THE SOURCE MATERIALS AVAILABLE?

Yes. Some of the materials are available. Original, digital artwork can be provided to organizations that have signed "Memorandum of Understanding" with The "I Love U Guys" Foundation.

Please note: Currently, original artwork is only provided in Mac OS X, Pages version 10.0 or QuarkXPress 2019 (15.2.1).

CAN YOU SEND ME MATERIALS IN MICROSOFT WORD?

The Public Address Poster, and all MOUs and NOIs are produced in Word. The other materials are not. Retaining the graphic integrity of the materials proved beyond our capabilities using Microsoft Word.

CAN I REALLY USE THE MATERIALS? WHAT ABOUT COPYRIGHTS AND TRADEMARKS?

Schools, districts, departments, agencies and organizations are free to use the materials under the "Terms of Use" outlined in this document and in the Memorandum of Understanding.

DO I NEED TO ASK PERMISSION TO USE THE MATERIALS?

No. You really don't need to ask permission. But, it would be great if you let us know that you're using our programs.

DO I HAVE TO SIGN AN MOU WITH THE FOUNDATION?

It is not necessary to sign an MOU with the Foundation, but please consider it. The Foundation is committed to providing programs at no cost. Yet, program development, enhancement, and support are cost centers for us. One way we fund those costs is through private grants and funding.

An MOU is a strong demonstration of program validity and assists us with these types of funding requests.

When you submit a completed MOU or NOI, you will be added to our database and notified when updates and new materials are available.

DO I HAVE TO SEND A NOTICE OF INTENT?

In the absence of an MOU, a Notice of Intent provides similar value to us regarding demonstrations of program validity to potential funders. Either one means that you will receive notification of updates and new materials.

DO I HAVE TO NOTIFY YOU AT ALL THAT I AM USING THE SRP?

We often speak with school safety stakeholders who have implemented the SRP but haven't mentioned it to us. Please let us know that your school, district, department or agency is using the SRP.

It is our goal that the SRP becomes the "Gold Standard." The more schools, districts, departments and agencies that we can show are using the program, the greater the chance for achieving our goal of having clear communication in a crisis.

CAN I PUT OUR LOGO ON YOUR MATERIALS?

Yes. But with some caveats. If you are a school, district, department or agency you may include your logo on posters and handouts. If you are a commercial enterprise, please contact us in advance with intended usage.

In some states, we have co-branding agreements with "umbrella" organizations (school district insurance pools, school safety centers, etc.). In those states, we ask that you also include the umbrella organization's branding.

WE WOULD LIKE TO PUT THE MATERIALS ON OUR WEBSITE.

Communication with your community is important. While you are free to place any material on your website, it's preferable that you link to the materials from our website. The reason for this is to allow us to track material usage. We can then use these numbers when we seek funding.

But, don't let that be a show stopper. If your IT group prefers, just copy the materials to your site.

DOES THE SRP WORK WITH "RUN, HIDE, FIGHT?"

In 2014, the Department of Education suggested "Run, Hide, Fight" as the preferred response to an active shooter. We don't believe the practice is mutually exclusive to the SRP, as that is a single-incident response. Again, consult with local law enforcement regarding your specific active shooter response.

There may be some challenges regarding training students using some of the "Run, Hide, Fight" materials. The Department of Education states "These videos are not recommended for viewing by minors."

DOES THE SRP WORK WITH A.L.I.C.E.?

Again, we don't believe that SRP and A.L.I.C.E. (single incident response) are mutually exclusive.

DOES THE SRP WORK WITH "AVOID, DENY, DEFEND?"

The SRP attempts to be an all-hazards approach to school based events. Of all of the active shooter responses, our determination is that "Avoid, Deny, Defend" from Texas State University has the best positioning, linguistics and actions. This response was created for adults and is for use in workplaces.

http://www.avoiddenydefend.org

DRILLS
FEMA Guidance

APPENDIX A - FEMA GUIDANCE

FEMA provides a description of each exercise and drill. The following information is from FEMA resources. The chart on the right page is their Building Block chart, and the descriptions here are how FEMA describes what each one entails, and the expected outcomes.

For in-depth learning, see IS-120.C: An Introduction to Exercises: (https://training.fema.gov/is/courseoverview.aspx?code=is-120.c)

DISCUSSION-BASED EXERCISES

SEMINAR

Seminars orient participants to or provide an overview into strategies, plans, policies, or procedures. Seminars can be valuable when an entity is developing new plans or making changes to existing plans or procedures.

Goals
- Orient participants to new or existing plans, policies, or procedures
- Research or assess interagency capabilities or inter-jurisdictional operations
- Construct a common framework of understanding

Characteristics
- Casual atmosphere
- Minimal time constraints
- Lecture-based

WORKSHOP

Workshops are more structured than seminars. Participant attendance and collaboration from relevant stakeholders is essential to obtain consensus and produce effective plans, procedures, and agreements.

Goals
- Develop a written product as a group, in coordinated activities
- Obtain consensus
- Collect or share information

Characteristics
- Broad attendance by relevant stakeholders
- Conducted based on clear objectives/goals
- More participant discussion than lecture-based seminar
- Frequently uses break-out sessions to explore parts of an issue with similar groups

Outcomes
- Emergency Operations Plans (EOPs)
- Mutual Aid Agreements
- Standard Operations Procedures (SOPs)

TABLETOP EXERCISE (TTX)

Tabletop exercises facilitate conceptual understanding, identify strengths, and areas for improvements, and/or achieving changes in perceptions. Participants are encouraged to problem-solve together through in-depth discussion. An effective TTX comes from active participants and their assessment of recommended revisions to current plans, policies, and procedures. It is important to have a facilitator keep the participants focused on the exercise objectives.

Goals
- Enhance general awareness
- Enhance roles and responsibility understanding
- Validate plans and procedures
- Rehearse concepts and/or assess types of systems in a defined incident

Characteristics
- Requires an experienced facilitator
- In-depth discussion
- Low stress, problem-solving environment

GAME

A simulation of operations that often involves two or more teams, usually in a competitive environment, using rules, data, and procedures designed to depict an actual or hypothetical situation. Identifying critical decision-making points is a major factor in the success of games.

Goals
- Explore decision-making processes and consequences
- Conduct "what-if" analyses of existing plans
- Evaluate existing and potential strategies

Characteristics
- No actual resources used
- Often involves two or more teams
- Includes models and simulations on increasing complexity as the game progresses
- May include pre-scripted messages

BUILDING BLOCK APPROACH TO EXERCISE SCHEDULING AND PLANNING

Full Scale Exercises

Functional Exercises

Games

Drills

Tabletops

Workshops

Seminars

Capability →

Planning and Training →

OPERATIONS-BASED EXERCISES

DRILL

A drill is a coordinated, supervised activity usually employed to validate a specific function or capability in a single agency organization. Drills are commonly used to provide training on tasks specific to new equipment or procedures, to introduce or validate procedures, or practice and maintain current skills.

Goals

- Provide training on new equipment
- Evaluate new procedures, policies, and/or equipment
- Practice and maintain skills
- Prepare for more complex exercises

Characteristics

- Immediate feedback
- Realistic but isolated environment

FUNCTIONAL EXERCISE (FE)

These are designed to validate and evaluate capabilities, multiple functions and/or sub-functions, or interdependent groups of functions. FEs are typically focused on exercising plans, policies, procedures, and staff members involved in management, direction, command, and control functions.

Goals

- Validate and evaluate capabilities
- Focused on plans, policies, and procedures

Characteristics

- Conducted in a realistic, real-time simulated environment
- Simulated deployment of resources and personnel
- Use of SimCell and Master Scenario Events List (MSEL)
- Include controller and evaluators

FULL-SCALE EXERCISE (FSE)

Full-scale exercises (FSE) are high stress multi-agency, multi-jurisdictional activities designed to test coordinated responses and rapid problem solving skills. These are the most complex, resource-intensive, and possibly expensive exercises.

Goals

- Demonstrate roles and responsibilities as addressed in plans and procedures
- Coordinate between multiple agencies, organizations and jurisdictions

Characteristics

- High-stress environment
- Rapid problem solving
- Critical thinking
- Conducted in a realistic, real-time environment to mirror a real incident
- Mobilization of units, personnel, and equipment

Made in the USA
Middletown, DE
20 August 2024